TALES *of a* DARKENED MIND

TALES *of a* DARKENED MIND

Shela Hutchinson

Columbus, Ohio

The views and opinions expressed in this book are solely those of the author and do not reflect the views or opinions of Gatekeeper Press. Gatekeeper Press is not to be held responsible for and expressly disclaims responsibility of the content herein.

Tales of a Darkened Mind

Published by Gatekeeper Press
2167 Stringtown Rd, Suite 109
Columbus, OH 43123-2989
www.GatekeeperPress.com

Copyright © 2021 by Shela Hutchinson
All rights reserved. Neither this book, nor any parts within it may be sold or reproduced in any form or by any electronic or mechanical means, including information storage and retrieval systems, without permission in writing from the author. The only exception is by a reviewer, who may quote short excerpts in a review.

The interior formatting, typesetting, and editorial work for this book are entirely the product of the author. Gatekeeper Press did not participate in and is not responsible for any aspect of these elements.

Library of Congress Control Number: 2021946065

ISBN (paperback): 9781662918834
eISBN: 9781662918841

Mentions

Edited by: Stacy Reppel

If you enjoy how good the grammar is or the way the book reads, and you need editing help for a project of your own. Please email her at:

stacy.reppel711@gmail.com

Illustrations:

All illustrations in the book are artworks produced by B. Wirthman. All work has been copyrighted and has Certificates of Authenticity. If you would like to contact her to do work for you, please email her at:

embracedartistry@gmail.com

The chibi art on the back cover was done by **dollmaker_**and can be found on Fiverr.

All other cover art was done by Shela Hutchinson, AKA Misfits and Lollipops. The work has been copyrighted and has a Certificate of Authenticity. Please use my alias find me on the following social medias, Facebook, Twitter, Instagram, Snapchat, YouTube, and Tumbler.

This book is dedicated to my son. I couldn't be more grateful to the love, light and hope you have brought into my life.

Prologue

In this book there are eight tales. Each tale is something different, but all connected by one thing, my own mind. Many things have been given life. In some cases a world of its own…all of it nestled inside my head. Things like monsters, thoughts, facades and voices have all been given a form. These things live in places like perfectly constructed prisons, an empty room with many doors, or even pure darkness. Fortunately for you there are lessons to be learned, which means other things have been given life. You'll see how hope regrows from its ashes, light can come through the darkness in unexpected ways, and that being honest with yourself can open your eyes to amazing things that were always there. Read through these tales with an open heart and mind. Reflect on yourself or possibly a loved one as you travel through each realm. Then, hopefully you understand yourself, or someone else, just a little bit better.

Lost in The Dark

In this first tale, we enter a world of darkness. A place so dark that seeing is impossible, making it incredibly difficult to move through the maze of life. We will see how it breaks a person down, making them feel as though there is no way out. How everything can come to a head in one moment, and how that moment can be the end of everything or a new beginning. Let us have this part of the mind that handles this tell their story and show you themselves.

I'm wandering through the dark: sometimes running, walking, or just stumbling. Sometimes I just sit in despair wondering if there is an end to the perpetual dark, then I will wish for the light. The light I remember from a time when I wasn't surrounded by the never ending dark that I am submersed in now. The memories from that time are getting fuzzy and hard to recall, but from what I can remember, it was bright and beautiful. I wish I could go back to relive those times, maybe stopping myself from ending up here in the dark. I know I need to keep moving forward and not look back on what once was. It's so dark that I can't seem to move forward, but I have to try, right? Walking, wandering, and lost in the dark, and feeling completely alone. There is a voice that echoes in the darkness. The voice speaks words of hate and anger that echo around me, solidifying and reinforcing what is being said. I listen because it's the only thing there consistently during my constant loneliness. Sometimes this voice is just too much. Being lost in the dark is just too much. Clawing for a way out, slamming into walls, stumbling on objects that I cannot see, and screaming at the top of my lungs for help…it all just becomes too much.

But I can't just end my life…even though the voice tells me I don't deserve the life I have. There are people that love me: my friends, my family. I just can't disappoint them. So, I drink alcohol and it makes the dark not so dark by turning the darkness into a blur. I smoke from a green plant that makes me not even care that it's dark, that I am alone and then I almost forget that it's dark as the smoke fills my entire being. Even though these things only have a temporary effect, it makes it easier to see, hear, and remember these people in my life that I don't deserve. Maybe then they could help lead me out of the darkness and into the light. I know that's where they are. The beautiful sound of their incredible voices ring in the darkness like the most amazing music you could ever hear. They also bring in little lights, sometimes high up like stars burning small holes through the darkness and flitting by like fireflies that dance around me and grace my skin with their glow. The drinking and the smoking don't feel so needed when this happens, but it never lasts long enough. If only these moments could last longer, I might be able to get out of here if they did.

There are lights that hurt though. Sometimes when wandering in the dark lanterns show up out of nowhere, a burning warm glow that casts ghostly shadows all around. The voice tells me not to bother, that I don't deserve it, that I am not good enough, and to just walk past. But I can't, I must hold onto it, so I do. I grab on for dear life, the brightest light I have seen in so long that I have almost forgotten what seeing really is. It's attached to…a wall? That means it can't move with me, so I have to stay in place. I still hold onto the lantern, as it whispers sweet nothings to hypnotize me further into a false safety that it creates. But the whispers never drown out the sound of the voice that tells me that I am worthless and undeserving of this dim glow that stands out in the perpetual darkness. Holding onto the lantern then starts to burn my hands. I welcome the pain it brings, because I haven't felt anything since the previous lantern that had come out of the darkness. Being alone with just the voice and the darkness can be so numbing to the entirety of my being. So, I just sit and take in the smell of the burning wick inside. I watch the flame dance hypnotically, while the flickers cause shivers to go down my spine as they continue the whispers, I strain to hear every word, pulling me into a deep hypnosis that starts to dull the pain. I just want to be lost in this world that is the lantern. It's not dark and I could feel only warmth every day. Then, the voice starts screaming at me so it can destroy the trance I am in. It screams disgusting profanities and degrading phrases that I can't ignore because they aren't wrong. I just can't let go. I start to feel the pain again, as it grows in intensity. I need to dull the pain myself, because the voice won't let me enter the trance again. I start to drink and smoke with urgency so I can't feel the pain. I just want to hold on longer. Even though I know that I have been holding on for too long already, I know I need to move on and keep moving forward. But the dark is so dark, and the loneliness is just too lonely, so I do everything I can to push past the pain. I continue to hold on to this light that I should never have grabbed. I know these lanterns are not good for me, but I just can't be alone in the dark anymore. Then the pain that was once welcomed, now is too much. I feel nothing as my nerves are too damaged to let me feel any sensation. I must let go, as the lantern starts to fade. My exhausted muscles have a deep soreness, and my heart is completely numb. Reluctantly, I let go and watch the light finally burn out.

It will be a long time before another one comes, and it feels so much longer between each and every time. So, I lay there, sore but numb, broken and burned, completely drained of energy. I can't and don't want to move forward. The prospect of another lantern is terrifying, but I know I'll hope for one, which is even scarier because it always happens the same way every time. When I hope for it, it's like I never learned anything, and the cycle never ends. Always being hurt by whatever throws those dangerous lanterns into the mix. The one positive is the voice leaves me alone during these times; it knows it can't hurt me more than I am already hurting myself. When the voice isn't there, my friends and family come through a little easier than before. They work to fill my ears with their beautiful sound and send their light to dance over my skin, also trying to fill what would be my sky with beautiful stars. Even though not all of it makes it through, I know they are still there somewhere, and I can try to find them. So, I pick myself up, dust myself off and start to walk forward again, letting time leave scars, just so I can find them again. I just want to be able to stand with them in the light. I am so tired of the voice, the darkness and everything that comes with it.

The exhaustion I feel has been engulfing me now. If I am not numb, I am completely sore from head to toe. Drinking and smoking becomes very regular. I just want to dull the pain or feel something when I am numb, but I have to keep moving forward. I have to try and find the end. These things may cloud my judgement, but they give me the ability to continue moving forward and I have to keep moving forward. I have just come to the realization that I am not moving forward to find the end for myself. I think that I have always known this. So many years in the dark made me want to believe that I was doing this for myself, but I am not. I have always moved forward for them: my friends, my family, the beautiful sounds and graceful lights. That is what I have been moving forward for, and those lights and sounds have been coming less and less. It's like they aren't there anymore. Will they be on the other side waiting for me?

The voice says, "No," continuing with a scoff, "Why would they be there?"

I answer, "They have been there for so long, they made music happen in the dark, and sent me lights for hope, they have to be there."

"You know you don't deserve them, why hope that they are there?" the voice says.

I say, "They worked so hard to give me hope. I can't just give up on them, I can't disappoint them."

"You have disappointed them. You're a burden. You leech off of them to continue a life you don't deserve." The voice scolded.

I can't say the voice is wrong. I can't argue. I have been here for so long and I keep running to the end of the dark for what? People who would be better off without me there, a life that I don't deserve, and the beautiful light of my childhood that might not be there? I can't go on. The future is too dark and bleak, and the memories I cherished have almost completely vanished. I have nothing fond to look back on. There have been no lanterns in so long: nothing from my friends and family, no more lights or sounds coming through, the voice more fever pitched. I am so numb that even the voice can't hurt me anymore. The dark is becoming all I have known and all that will be there. Drinking and smoking have no effect anymore, no matter how much I take in. I slam into walls, fall to the ground, and it gets harder and harder to get up every time. They aren't waiting. There is nothing anymore, so I just sit alone in the dark, with only the voice for company.

As I am sitting and drinking alone, I come up with a plan, to finally end this dark. I will finally be free of the voice that torments me so. I quietly put in the final decision to grab a bottle of pills. The decision to leave without making a sound, letting the world in the light, stay in the light. I finally feel free as the bottle of pills opens up outside. The smell of medication fills the dark void around me and this feels familiar. I have been here before. There have been other bottles of pills, but it was never real, not like it is now. This time is different.

*This time was different, what this part of my mind can't tell you is what I had done on the outside, in the real world. I snuck past people I lived with, people I loved and cared about. A bottle of pills, and a jug of a mixed drink as my weapon. I left the place I lived, ready to not ever come back. I walked to a place where no one would know me when I was found. I brought the edge of the bottle to my lips and told myself to tip it back so I could take in the product into my being and end the perpetual darkness. The voice echoed through my head, "**Do it. You have lived a life you don't deserve long enough. You don't deserve those people you love; you have burdened them long enough.**" I kept the bottle to my lips, I was ready to take the plunge, I stopped. A message from a friend. The ding my phone made reverberated through my whole body. I stopped listening to the voice, I stopped what I was doing, and set the bottle down next to my* *empty jug. I just sat for a time, staring at the phone, being deafened by silence. While something happened in the darkness...*

There is a sound that stops my chance at freedom. The sound is a shockwave I can't understand the purpose of. Then there was nothing but my complete darkness, and a crushing soundlessness that makes me unable to move. Then, I screamed. I scream so loud that the voice can't speak over me. I screamed so loud that the darkness shook. I scream so loud that some higher power heard me. I heard a new voice... my voice? Is that my **real** voice speaking to me? I have never heard my own voice before, but it's telling me to get up. It's telling me to move, and that even though trust is hard to do, I have to trust them now. That I have to trust my own instinct and keep walking. The voice came back screaming, but I did as I was told and moved, the voice screaming the entire time. I kept walking, ignoring the voice that wasn't mine, and soon there was a lantern. It looked familiar, but there was a feeling that I shouldn't hold on. That I needed to walk past and leave it behind, like I should have done so many times before. So, I do just that. I walk up to it but don't latch on, looking past it, I see a path, and start walking down it, watching the lantern behind me fade out until everything is dark again. I start to think that I did the wrong thing. I should have stayed.

I should have held on, as the dark was all consuming again.

I couldn't drink or smoke and I wish I had made a different decision. I am still in the dark and still completely alone. I started to feel like my own voice lied to me. The voice was doing everything to validate that feeling and telling me that I didn't deserve to even exist. My instinct told me to keep going. That there was something, so I kept moving and that's when everything changed.

A brightly lit torch came to fruition in my hand. It glittered under its own light, and its glow felt so warm. It cast a bright light, so bright that it lit the whole area around me, showing me that I was in a tunnel. That is when hope welled up within me. All tunnels have an end, right? I knew then that I was in a labyrinth of tunnels, and it was always too dark for me to see. The voice tells me to pass the torch to someone who deserves it more than me, but I can't just leave it. The torch needs me, it wants me, and I can't just give up on it. My family and friends are coming through with their lights and sounds, showing me that they have always been there, but the darkness and the voice made it too hard for them to reach me. I know now what I must do. I must keep moving forward. I crawl, walk, run, sprint, and anything else

I can do to keep moving forward so I can find the end. I stumble sometimes, run into walls, find dead ends, and just get plain lost, but I keep holding on. I keep moving forward. The voice still tries to get me to end my life and make me feel horrible about myself. But it's easier to tune the voice out and just listen to the good things that everyone sends in and see the torch that has brought me hope.

All I can say now, from all that I have learned, is that if you are lost in the dark like me and have hit the point when you stop and can't move forward anymore, the point where ending your life is the only thing that makes sense, just scream. Scream for help. Scream as loud as you can. Scream till your lungs give out. Be heard by the higher power that helps you, or the person that comes in, and listen to your voice that follows. Start the journey that brings you your torch, because you matter, you have worth, and you deserve your torch. You may still be lost in the dark, but at least there is hope for an end. Being without hope for your own life is incredibly debilitating. Restoring your hope is the first step to finding the end of the dark. I know how hard it is to trust anything but let your instinct, your **real** voice, lead you out. You may even have fun on the way to finding your torch.

There are many things to be learned from this story. This story from the darkened part of my mind and myself may resonate with you in some way, and that is ok. It is ok to be in the dark, you only need to know how to get out. You may need something in your arsenal to help you get out, so just remember, chapters always end, but it doesn't always mean the end of the story.

Finding My Torch

With this glorious tale we see exactly how the experiences life has to offer can affect us in strange and incredible ways. We find what may be an amazing experience for one is not always the case for another. This journey I had was difficult for me, but I would never change a moment of it. Let's start from the beginning to truly learn what I mean.

The knowledge of a growing life inside of me hit me like a ton of bricks. I never felt as though this could be real, and I knew I didn't deserve a miraculous new life. All I could feel about my situation was that I stole this child from the stars above and out of the hands of someone who deserved this kind of love. It wasn't only that I didn't deserve this, I couldn't do this. I couldn't keep my own life together long enough to support another life. I have never been self-sufficient, and in this short time being unable to self-medicate is already tearing me apart. I couldn't find the strength to move off the couch with these debilitating thoughts, and nothing around me had brought any solace. I had to let this new reality sink in though; I needed to make a decision. *Do I keep what I don't deserve or give this life to someone that does?*

This someone would deserve the responsibility of growing a life and they would survive without help. They would be self-sufficient, and dependable. They would be able to hold their life together with grace and would not need the help of self-medicating. I had no idea how I would do this. I also never really wanted the responsibility because I always believed that I couldn't take care of another human life. Then this moment came, where I was faced with the possibility, and I still couldn't make myself believe that I was capable of raising a small human. The person, who deserved to raise a newborn into an adult, would not only believe they could; the responsibility would be everything they could have ever dreamed of and so much more. I didn't have the strength to love myself. I have never believed in my ability to do anything, and I couldn't find the energy to even move off of the couch to care for myself. How would I be able to do everything that was needed for someone who would need me to do everything for them? Someone who truly deserved this responsibility would be able to love themselves enough to love selflessly. They would believe that they could do all that was needed and more for that little life. They would have the energy to do all the things that are necessary. The people around me instantly thought I would keep this being without a second thought. They became angry when I brought up my idea of giving this child to someone who really deserved a child, their anger made it incredibly hard to decided. My disbelief that this fetus was even real made the decision even more difficult.

When I finally went in for the first ultrasound, it gave me a little hope that I would ultimately be able to make a decision. I hoped that it will finally make all of this real for me. I hoped that it would calm the people around me so I could think for myself. I hoped for an answer to all of my questions and a final decision to the choice that I had to make. All of my hopes were dashed the moment I looked at the screen. I just got more questions and I was too afraid to ask them out loud. The ultrasound showed the being trapped inside of me; it was an alien being not of this world. It also kind of reminded me of a kidney bean. So maybe, it was an alien from a world where everything and everyone was made of beans? It really was very strange. Yeah, I couldn't do this; I couldn't even see the life growing inside of me as human. How could I care for it the way I needed to? Everyone around me kept telling me that I would be a good mom and that I should stop thinking about the alternative. I never believed them. They have been giving it cute nicknames in an effort to make me more comfortable with it. That's what I had felt about the names, it didn't really work though.

I continued to move on with time. There was puking, pain, soreness, and more puking. This has been really uncomfortable, and I was alone through most of it. Alone at night with thoughts like: *I don't deserve a life with joy and laughter.* Alone, during the day, with the pain and soreness of just existing daily. I was always completely alone with the question of whether to keep it or give it away gnawing away at my neurons. Then one day, I felt it move. The strangest feeling I ever experienced, and I didn't know how to share it with anyone. I couldn't form a real thought, other than: *I feel a foreign being inside of my body moving* and *I have no idea how to handle this.* There was still no connection but the physical one. I finally felt the being that was growing inside of me and it was leeching any spare nutrients I had plus some. It was definitely more real than it ever was. At that moment, I was terrified of how real it had become. It was all so real to me at that moment, and I still didn't have a connection to it in my mind or emotions. I even still call this living being an it! How could I keep this child when I couldn't connect to it?

People would tell me to do things with it like reading and listening to music, and I would finally see there is an unconditional love for the being inside me. So, I read out loud, and I included it in my music choices as best I could. It would move around a lot when we listened to Elvis. I wonder if that means they like **The King**. It has still felt so weird when it moves around, but I have to try and get used to it for the time being. I still wondered when the connection would happen. Maybe then the weird feeling of the movement would stop feeling so odd. Maybe then I wouldn't feel so conflicted. I tried so desperately to feel that connection that everyone keeps telling me will happen, and it didn't ever happen for me. *Is it because this child doesn't belong to me? Maybe that's what was wrong with the whole situation, this being growing inside of me doesn't truly belong to me. That means I have to give this unborn child to someone, the person that it belongs to. The people around me tell me that I shouldn't, that I can't, but what if it is the right thing to do?*

I had another ultrasound coming up, and a new hope that I would finally find that connection. As I lay on the bed looking at the screen as the tech took measurements of the life growing inside me, it looked more like a human than the last time: a face, hands, feet, but still no connection. I wanted to cry but I didn't, I didn't want to explain why I was crying to the person with me in the room. On the way home I stared at the picture trying to find the connection.

As I sat in my bedroom I cried because I couldn't find it; I couldn't feel it. I decided that I would continue trying. Then if by the time this being came into the world, the physical connection gone, and still nothing else there, I would do the right thing. I continued to read out loud every night and still included it in my music choices. I watched the television a little louder than normal, and it moved a lot when the Friends theme music played. *Seriously, does that mean they like it? I hope so because this still felt weird.* I thought of other ways to try and make the pregnancy better and I think I got it. I decided to continue to leave the gender a secret to give me a surprise for later. *I do love a good surprise and this one is a really big surprise.*

I had heard how people would have this beautiful connection with their fetus. I tried so hard to experience what they felt and nothing worked for me. I wanted this miraculous link to happen for me, as time went on, the connection seemed more and more like fiction. The only correlations I made was how swollen my feet were, how much my back hurt, and how tired I was. As the end inched ever closer, all I could think was, *I just want this to be over so my body can go back to some semblance of normalcy.* I would have taken the place I was before, the painful numbness, constant self-deprecation, and the feeling of death that covered me. I could have continued to endure all of that over everything that happened at that point. I would cry for no reason, I was more sore than normal, and I felt more alone than I ever had, even though I had been carrying a growing human life with me everywhere. *I can't stop thinking about how awful I feel, and how I don't deserve a full life and a child, maybe I really should look into giving this being to someone who truly deserves this.* There was no connection to my fetus, this magical connection everyone talked about, it felt like the universe tried to tell me that this child wasn't mine. Thoughts relentlessly ran through my head, and spiraled downward, like never ending train tracks with constant derailments.

If I feel this alone while it is attached to me, what will I feel when it finally isn't. Why do I keep calling it an it! I can't even gather myself for work, how am I going to take care of a whole other person? What is wrong with me? If only I could be normal. Now my back hurts from trying to tie my shoes, this is ridiculous, and now I am crying like an idiot. Why did I have to get pregnant? Just why? Now I am crying harder, what the hell. I have so many things to do, and I can't get my act together long enough to do anything. I think I may just lay on the couch, probably a safe bet. No, if I am going to do anything I have to get off the couch. Why can't I just do things like regular people, right, I am pregnant and don't want to be. I feel like I am as big as a house, my feet are swollen, and I am so sore that moving is just impossible. I honestly…I don't think I can do this. No, I know I can't do this. If this is all I can feel, if this is all I can think, then I shouldn't do this and I will have to do the right thing. I was completely alone with all these thoughts, afraid to talk to those around me. I didn't know what to do, I didn't know how to go about doing what was right, and the loneliness that ate at every fiber of my being.

The time had finally arrived, the nine months were up, and I was scared shitless. Everyone that was home was getting up, nerves were on high alert, and my ability to walk was slowly being drained. I make it to the car, and what is about a five-minute drive to make it to the hospital, felt like an eternity. Walking into the hospital was a laborious task, but when I walk through the hospital doors, and describe the problem, I get offered a wheelchair. I am brought to a room where nurses, the doctor, and people that had come there to support me were asking me questions and talking to me. I was angry with everyone because I was in so much pain. I felt like a stray dog, biting at everyone that came near me. I wanted this to be over at that very moment, every minuet felt like hours, the pain was agonizing and I knew it was only going to get worse. I closed my eyes in an attempt to go to another place. A place where the excruciating pain didn't exist, a better mindset that made everything easier, and to a time where the right decision was already made. The doctor and nurses tried telling me things to try and expedite the process, and everything they told me to do hurt more than it needed to. When the afternoon finally arrived, I was told that I needed to push this being out, but I didn't want to. All this pain and it still had not come out. I knew the pain was going to get worse and I was not prepared. Everyone around me kept me there to go through this, to finally finish what was started, and I was not ready. Muscles reacted and started to work on their own. They operated in unison to move this being through each agonizing stage of birth. After the indescribable pain of pushing a small human being out of my body, I heard the words, "It's a boy!" Then they laid him on me. He was covered in fluids and blood; his skin felt sticky with it. I patted his back and poked at him, checking that he was at least alive, but I really wanted him to be moved off of me. I couldn't really see him, and I wanted to at least look at him before I decided. I felt so tired and could barely move when they finally had my mother cut the umbilical cord and then moved him over to check his vitals among other things.

I laid in my hospital bed, with no energy after the excruciating pain I just went through, I looked over to finally see him. I needed to look him in the eyes, he at least deserved that before I said that he never belonged to me. So, I moved my head to face him and whatever possible future that awaited me. That was when it finally hit me. I saw his face was turned towards me, his eyes were open and looking directly into my soul. I felt him look passed the walls I had built, and the façade that I had put on. It was like he could see me, all of me. It didn't seem to faze him at all that I was damaged. The darkness that was consuming me, the words that constantly berated me, thoughts that threatened to drown me, and my soul shattered from years of torment. None of it mattered to him. He didn't care that I was going to be his whole world for a while, he just wanted and needed me there. Then my heart that has felt cold and broken for so long was touched by light. I could feel love, understanding and peace wash over me. It was almost as if we had met before, in another life, and he was brought back to help me again like he had so many times before, by being my child again. The connection was finally made.

I know that I am not going to be the best mom. I know I am going to fail a lot. I also know that I am going to try. The greatest moment of my life was the moment he was brought into my life. I now know that he was put in my life because I screamed so many months ago for help. My need for a reason to move forward so I can find the light at the end of my tunnel. For him, I will continue my journey. My beautiful son is the torch to light the dark I have been lost in for so long. No matter the ups and downs of the journey to find my torch, I will never regret it.

Now listen very carefully. You may not have the same journey, your torch may be totally different, but I recommend you take the journey to find it. Find who or whatever it is, and I promise you won't regret it.

The Flood

This part of the mind sends their tale as a message in a bottle. Unable to leave their confines to be able to tell it themselves. I am truly honored to be the one to read it to you all. To really feel this story, we need to start with a clear and open mind, as we enter a world with no rhyme or reason, and drowning without water, we will need room for understanding.

To whom that finds this, read carefully…

Standing in an empty room, letting a feeling of calm wash over me, I don't have the opportunity to feel like this very often. This room is not normally empty or calm. So, I do what I can to enjoy the peace when it comes. In my humble room there are no windows, however, there are many doors that completely encircle me. I can't see outside to know what is happening, and no one can see in so I can signal for help. I don't dare to open those doors, because they let in the uncontrollable madness that could drive anyone insane. I keep my eyes closed so I don't have to look at them, and I don't go anywhere near them. All because I cannot bear the absolute chaos that comes through those doors now.

There was a period of time, seemingly forever ago, when I could have conversations with the thoughts that waltzed through those doors. We could speak in a civilized manner, using facts, opinions, and morals to come to sensible solutions. Then voices would chime in as if over a loudspeaker. They would conversate with all of us to make a final decision, then they take and use that decision somewhere else. When everything worked like this, things got done. Now, nothing gets done.

Those voices ringing throughout the room, but never seen, call themselves the conscience and the subconscious. The conscience is okay. It's kind of bland, bossy at times, and all about right and wrong. Even with all its boring, black and white thinking, I still like it more than the subconscious. The subconscious is very dark, rather scary, and is ready to do anything with its drastic ideas that can help… sometimes.

During a simpler time, the conscience was the one that usually prevailed by leading the thoughts and I with rational thought and a deep sense of integrity. The subconscious only won when extreme measures needed to be taken. That is how it should work, but for a while everything has been different, and has not happened like that. Something changed the way the thoughts operate. After the interference happened, the thoughts interacted with everything differently, altering the dynamics of the conscience and subconscious, nothing has been the same ever since.

The thoughts come in on their own; it's like the doors are broken. The doors open freely, allowing the thoughts to scurry in like a large hoard of rats. They claw over and trample each other as they flood into my space. The doors will not close on their own to stop the uncontrollable mob. I try to force the doors closed on my own, but too many thoughts running in like an overflowing river, make it impossible to do that. Then, there are too many thoughts in my room, they have to scream to be heard over each other. Neither of the voices can be heard since there are no breaks in the screaming thoughts. Nothing can be done and decisions can't be made, because the thoughts aren't communicating with one another. Then, they start fighting with each other. The movement around me feels like giant rogue waves crashing into each other during a storm, and I was the sinking ship. The screaming and fighting make it impossible to think about the next move. As the thoughts bloody each other, the conscience tries to speak over them. It tries to tell them to stop and work together. It doesn't work no matter how much the conscience repeats itself. Then, more thoughts pour in. There is more screaming and fighting. I can't close the doors as the thoughts crash in like the ocean's waves. There is so much going on, and nothing is getting done.

Too many thoughts have been screaming and fighting. There is no room to move, and I fall to my knees as I give up on trying to close the doors. I get trampled by the plethora of thoughts that have filled this room beyond its capacity. I can't breathe, no words can come out, and everything around me is turning into a whirlwind of insanity. I can barely hear the conscience as it screams,

"Stop! We need to work together! Stop fighting!"

I know the thoughts didn't hear it because they didn't stop. I'm not strong enough to stand and help contain the madness surrounding me. I still can't breathe, as tears stream down my face. My last-ditch attempt in begging for it all to stop. I can only hear the screaming, as it pierces so deep that covering my ears doesn't even muffle it. I feel the thumps of each hit as the thoughts fight each other. That's when the subconscious speaks, like a whisper only I can hear. It whispers only one word,

"Pain."

It speaks so sweet and smooth like honey dripping off its wicked tongue. As it repeats itself, I try to tell myself that I can't. I really don't want to; I never do but I always end up giving in to the repeated demands that the subconscious gives.

   I start pulling my hair, scratching myself, and ripping at my face, anything I can do to cause pain. Finally shocked back into breathing, I scream at the top of my lungs. Continuing to pinch, rip, and bite at myself, causing me to screech and scream even louder. I could hear maniacal laughter coming from the subconscious, but the conscience says nothing. As if the conscience was absent to the scene that I knew was in front of them. Then, as suddenly as they all came, the thoughts were gone. The doors slam behind them leaving nothing but a body numbing silence. I lay in the middle of my, now empty, room curled up in the fetal position. Broken, battered, and bruised I cry. I cry tears of sadness and disappointment in myself. My disappointment falling to the failure of keeping control of the situation, yet again. Giving in to the demands that I hurt myself to stop the insanity causes my sadness. I wonder when this cycle of self-abuse will end and if I will ever have those peaceful conversations with the thoughts ever again. I am so tired, so sore, and I couldn't get up even if I wanted to. Leaving me to reminisce on older times, happier times, and wonder when they would come back.

   I think that the conscience is tired too because it doesn't ever talk anymore outside of yelling at the thoughts. It yells at the thoughts to stop what they are doing when they get out of control, and that is the only time I hear it speak now. What's worse is that the conscience is not making many decisions outside of this room, and the subconscious is taking advantage of the whole situation. The subconscious has been approving strange things, more frequently, as of late. A strange sickly-sweet liquid has been falling from the ceiling like rain, and weird smelling smoke clouds the air. These events signal a different set of thoughts to come in. I only see these thoughts walk through the doors when all of those events happen. The conscience starts to giggle, as if it has lost complete control of itself and I can feel the insidious grin of the subconscious as it beckons forth a 'party'. I don't understand how this is a party because I am not having any fun. The room becomes incredibly damp, and I can hardly breathe with all the smoke. These weird thoughts don't speak very well. Everything is slurred and they can't form a whole sentence. I really can't complain too much because they aren't screaming or fighting each other. Then it hits me, I become lightheaded and my vision blurs. I can barely take in their already incoherent speech. So, I just sit on the floor watching, as the thoughts pass by me, and the room starts to spin.

The conscience still giggles, and the subconscious starts excitedly accepting whatever the thoughts are saying. I can't believe that it understands what the thoughts are saying, but it has to, with the way that it accepts whatever these strange thoughts are saying. Then, out of nowhere, the subconscious sneaks into my head with its whisper,

"It's fine, I can take care of everything. Just rest."

I really shouldn't listen. I should stay awake and do my job, but I don't think I can anymore. I am getting really tired from all this smoke and the liquid raining down on me. So I just lay down. I mean, the subconscious can handle this, right? The subconscious wouldn't kill us, right? I can't really understand the thoughts anyway. What help would I be? Also, I don't care at this point, I am too tired to care what happens. As I close my eyes, I hear random mumblings from the thoughts, before I finally shut off, leaving the subconscious in full control.

When I finally turn back on, I am still kind of drowning in this strange liquid, but it's different now. I feel like I am floating in the ocean, waves rocking me back and forth, and the room has almost succumbed to the darkness that is my salvation. That means the dreams will play like movies, and I don't have to do anything. No thoughts can come in. I don't hear the voices of the conscience and subconscious. I can finally just sit back and relax. Outside this room, it's called sleep, but nothing really works. I don't have to deal with thoughts because it's almost like they don't exist. I think the conscience and subconscious work together to make dreams, so all I have to do is watch the dreams. Yes, sometimes they are nightmares, but anything is better than all the events that happen on a regular basis. If I could continuously stay in a dream, sleep would be all that happens outside of this room. Then I could just sit and watch my personal movies all the time, but, unfortunately, it can't ever be like that.

When the world outside wakes up, everything hurts. The room and I feel more dry than usual. I also feel really sore. This isn't going to be the last time I feel like this. It's not going to be the last time any of these things happen. This cycle seems endless. I don't know how to end this, and no one I know is helping me figure out how to fix anything. I know that I can't leave this room to find anything else out. So, I have to deal with the flood of thoughts coming in, screaming, and fighting each other, and the conscience being totally useless at this point. Then, the subconscious doing whatever the hell it wants with the fluid and smoke that forcibly fills my space. I don't know how long I can do this. This cycle doesn't seem to have an end. I can't fix or help whatever has broken or changed. I don't know if I can get help, or if there is help outside of this room.

I don't feel as if I have a purpose anymore. I played a part in the human mind that helped in making decisions for things that are said or done on the outside, but now I don't even feel like I am ever going to be able to do my job ever again. Is there help out there? Is there any way that I could make it possible to get help? I also wonder what you would do. If you are reading this, it means that I could finally get my message out. So I really want to know, what would you do if you were trapped in my position? Speak up, because I can't even think anymore.

Signed,

The thought process.

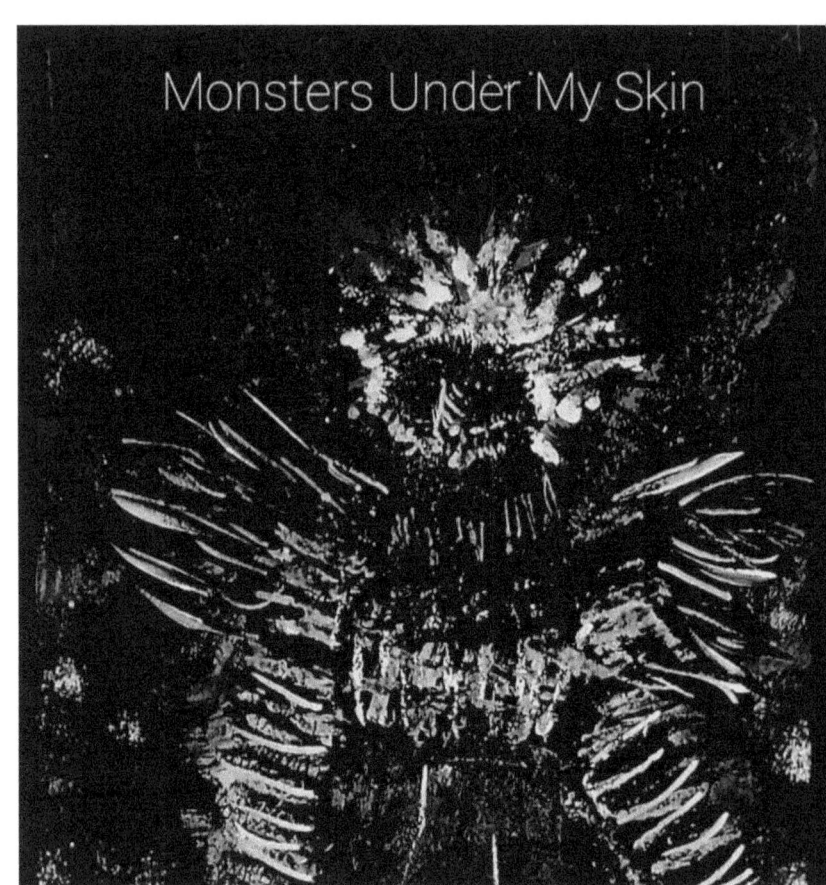

Monsters Under My Skin

With this tale, we enter a realm of monsters. Unlike most tales these monsters are real, and they can be found inside of human beings. They go by many names. Names like anger, frustration, distrust, and any other name you'd like to give them. To begin this tale, we have to ask ourselves a very important question.

Have you ever questioned if you were human?

For the story I am about to tell you I had to dig really deep to answer this question, so I could tell you this scary tale of monsters trapped in the darkest parts of myself.

There are times I'm pretty sure I am human, but the feeling that I am not is always lingering. There are…*things*, crawling underneath my skin, making me feel that I am not like everyone else. I do what I can to walk through life unnoticed. My skin keeps these things, what I can only call monsters, inside. These monsters are incredibly terrifying to me. I am still scared of them even though I have gotten used to them. I understand them, I know they are there and what they want, yet I am still petrified of what they could do. Their goal is to get out of the prison that was constructed with in me and I can't let that happen. People around me won't be able to understand these things. They will be horrified to know what is lurking underneath the surface. That's why I can't let people see what is hiding beneath my skin…they can't know how I am being taken over by awful things that I have lost control of.

They get riled up with many things…just normal, everyday things that everyone deals with. Something as simple as being at a job that you don't enjoy, and the people around you make it even worse. Having a slightly annoying conversation with someone. A person being absentmindedly rude and many other general misunderstandings going unresolved. All these things, and more, seem to feed these monsters. I never talk these things out with people when they happen. I just bottle up all the minor inconveniences, fearing that the monsters will escape if I don't. Capturing these moments, giving them no chance for escape, leaves the monsters to feed on them, until the issue is consumed. Then, the monsters keep it, letting the issue boil under their scales to make it bigger than the matter really is. Whether they are individuals from my social circle, someone I meet randomly during the day, or a person that is somewhere in between those two options.

These normal everyday annoying interactions can happen anytime, anywhere, with anyone. No matter who it is, I have to keep the monsters at bay, holding them prisoner underneath my skin.

Even though I try so hard to keep them confined, there are times that they scratch past the surface just a little bit. Just that small scratch can cause chaos. Out of nowhere, I will start screaming at people, people close to me, for no reason or faults of their own. I say things that I don't even believe or thought I had forgiven and forgotten. I can't feel anything as rage starts to boil over, fueled further by vile monsters in another attempt to fully escape. A small glimmer of fear creeps in to remind me how important it is to keep them in. I pivot in the argument with whoever is there to focus inward and try to keep the monsters at bay. The person I started screaming at continues the argument. They are angry with what I had said, and this anger then fuels the monsters even more. The monsters gobble it up as the frustration comes in. Telling them to stop arguing with me doesn't work. They can't stop, as the poisonous bite of the words that I couldn't help but speak, start to course through their veins. This is why I work so hard to keep them away from the world. There is an infectious negativity about them that spreads amongst whoever is there to take their abuse. I have to protect those that I hold in the highest regard because they are the ones that keep me grounded. Unfortunately, they are also the ones that experience the wrath of my monsters the most. These people spend so much time in my life that it is almost inevitable for them to be hurt by the monsters that live inside me.

Hurting these people was always the last thing that I wanted, but it's something that happened that I am still making up for. Keeping monsters couped up was not an easy task though, and there were times that I would let them out, because every warden has to take a brake and sleep sometime, right?

When I can be completely alone, I can finally let the monsters out. They claw out any way they can and wreak havoc along the way. An overall soreness covers me from head to toe due to the fact that I am fighting to keep them in all day. They run out of the deepest parts of my mind, and rush past my heart, ripping and tearing as they crawl and sprint from their holding cells. There are sharp pains in my muscles as they force their way out into a world that they don't belong. Black sludge pours out of my eyes like poisonous tears, burning their way down my cheeks, and dripping off my chin. The thick black liquid also drains out of my nose, ears and mouth as if I have turned into a broken faucet linked to a hellish well. This black ooze fills the space around me and releases a miasma that makes the air almost deadly to breathe. This is where the monsters can take a physical form outside of the prison that was made for them, that has been placed uncomfortably inside of me. They lurk and move about in the space I have allowed them to be, looking to feed on anything they can. Their main sources of food are anger, irritations and pain. When they are finally satisfied that it is just me and there is no one else to feed off of, they turn all of their focus towards me.

They grip my nerves with their awful talons and whisper deadly thoughts that swim through my ears and seep into my brain like venom. I have dealt with them for so long that they can't anger or annoy me anymore. They know that. The monsters know exactly how to farm their nourishment from me, by eliciting pain. They make me harm myself, in ways that seem strange, such as: scratching, cutting and burning my flesh. Never anything severe enough to kill me, but enough to leave scars. Adrenaline starts to course through my veins, making this not seem so bad, giving me a feeling of euphoria after the pain. The exhilaration is addicting. So I don't fight the control they have on me as much anymore. They feed off my pain, by breathing it in off my skin, as if pain were a pheromone released from my pores. I scratch open old wounds or cut and burn new ones. I can only stop when they are fully satisfied.

When they are finally appeased and I am bandaging my wounds, they swirl around me in an excited frenzy cheering with their fulfillment. I finally make it to my bed to sleep and I continue to let them be free in the space I provided them with, always in the hope that capturing them in the morning won't be so difficult. This approach never works, but I like to believe it helps. Sleep is my escape from everything that I have to deal with, and I don't have to be the warden of an internal prison that was created for these monsters. I can just dream or have nightmares. I have the ability to repair and relax in the comfort of a world that doesn't exist. Never prepared for what awaits me when I wake up. Daylight, hitting my eyes signals my mind and body to wake up. As I am sitting up, I know what comes next. I have to start throwing the monsters back to their holding cells, and it causes so much distress every time. I breath the miasma in deeply and let the sludge coat my skin to absorb it all. This forces the monsters back because I am the only place they can exist now. Rushing back to their prison through my ears, nose and mouth; tears rolling down my cheeks like waterfalls, as they push past each other, to make room in their prison. I take my place as the prison guard to keep the world safe again, and it causes a general soreness over my whole body that I cannot ever escape.

I stop letting them out every night, and I have been increasing the amount of time that I keep them locked up in their holding cells to stop all the pain. Maybe I can starve them. If I stop giving them things to feast on, maybe they will die off, or maybe just be good for a while. I am trying to feel completely numb to anything relating to the daily annoyances, trying to not hurt, or feel anger but I think this plan is failing too. When I look in the mirror, I start to see parts of the monsters as part of my own appearance, as if I am becoming one of them. Dark scales and spines and yellow eyes and sharp lines make up what I see. While I have been containing these monsters, I have been turning into one myself. I have no idea how to stop it. As I sit and contemplate my humanity, I wonder if I will ever feel fully human again. I wonder if I am the only one like me. I doubt the ability to get rid of these monsters and I want to try and find a way to live with them, but I am terrified that I might become one of them.

Now I am supposed to give you a lesson. I regret to inform you that not all stories are going to end with a proper lesson. I will, however, leave you with a question. This question is one that you have to answer for yourself if you are dealing with incomprehensible monsters like me. What happens if I become the monsters that I contain?

A Mask

*With this tale, we learn the simple ways that someone will hide in plain sight, and what it is like to do so. Putting on a disguise to show the world that we are '**just fine**', but in reality, we are being consumed by something that no one can actually see.*

Have you ever hidden yourself from the world? Have you ever huddled under a blanket, or nestled deep into a hoodie, so you could create a barrier between yourself and the world around you? Trust me, I get it. The world has so many problems, and it would make anyone want to hide. I can tell you; I hide every day. It's not quite in the ways I previously described, but I do put a barrier between me and the world. I have a mask that I put on every day. This mask makes me feel safe. It also keeps people from seeing the tragic story that I have become. No one knows what I am actually feeling or thinking. The sanity, I barely have a grasp on, or my ability to function in daily life is never questioned. Everyone thinks that I am okay; that is the way it needs to be. Anyone that will run into me is fooled by the mask I put on and keep close at hand.

This mask also comes in handy with deceiving my close friends and family. They are the ones that need to believe that everything is 'just fine' the most. All they will do is worry if they knew what was truly going on in the worlds hiding just past my eyes. I know that I will never be able to handle how upset they would be after seeing the hideous thing that I have become underneath my façade. Will they be hurt if they finally see everything I am concealing? *Probably.* They love me for some reason that I can't comprehend, therefore, I can't hurt them. These people in my life are incredible and I don't deserve the kindness and love they give me. I can only imagine what they would say or do if they found out what I am hiding from them. *They would probably wonder if there was anything that they could have done to prevent this from ever happening, blaming themselves for something that has no reason.* The thing is, I know nothing specific happened to give me this life of inner torment. Nothing could have been avoided to change everything that I have dealt with, or anything I will continue to endure. So, I wear this mask so they will continue to believe that everything is 'just fine'.

At this point, you are probably wondering what I am hiding behind this mask. I also know that you are probably thinking, 'it can't be that bad'. I am at the point now, where I can tell you, it is definitely not great. There is so much that I hide behind the mask. An incredible number of awful things that happened behind my disguise while I waltzed through life as if it were a masquerade. No one understood that it was all an elaborate performance.

Concealing myself behind this mask was like the curtains of a stage, obscuring all that the stagehands do to make the show flawless. Behind the scenes I cry alone in my perpetual darkness; my tears hitting nothing in this abyss. Constantly fumbling to find the next mark in the gloomy shadows of a world well hidden. A voice rings out from the darkness to yell belittling and profane things at me. Behind the mask I can cover my ears to try and block out all of its words. Though my attempts to deafen myself to the self-abuse of this voice from within always fail, I can still try. As thoughts rush into a space that should be guarded, I can scream and yell without anyone being the wiser to my actions. My shouts always going unanswered by rampaging thoughts, trampling everything in their path, leaving only chaos and indecision in their wake. Monsters crawl about, constantly waiting to feed on the unsuspecting victims around me. I can fight them without anyone knowing they even exist. I face an onslaught of horror as they rip deep into my soul and tatter the edges of my mind. My constant battle will keep them from spilling out and infecting the world. So much goes on behind this mask that no one knows about, and fear stops me from saying anything to anyone. I am constantly falling in a hellish abyss that was created to torture me and me alone. Since no one should see the suffering that was designed for me, I will keep my mask well fitted over my unfortunate reality. All anyone will ever know is the incredible show I perform every day.

This mask fits so well now that it does many things for me, so I don't have to even think about taking in the world outside. It talks for me, having wonderful conversations that I wouldn't be able to participate in normally. The normal, mundane, conversations about the weather or other dry, over thought topics happen with an ease and certainty that I wouldn't be able to provide. The deeper conversations happen with a more cunning precision that no one is aware of. My mask navigates the parts of my mind it needs to grab the information it needs to have a smooth flowing conversation, as I deal with dark torments. I display emotions to people around me when all I can truly feel is numbness or pain. Even though I know I do care, this mask has to show it for me; I can't face anyone to give them my true empathy. Moreover, this front can smile for me. All the smiles, grins, and smirks it flashes around tells everyone that I am okay. They see me laughing at jokes and joking about myself; no one will think that there is anything wrong. No one will ever worry about me and I cannot be more grateful to my mask. This mask can act its way through any situation better than I could try and live them.

There is so much that this mask has to cover, as I turn into a broken husk of my former self, that many would call damaged goods. I have been misplaced in a world of darkness, self-deprecation, monsters, and chaos. So far gone that I have been worn down to nothing but skin and bone inside the prison that is my mind. I have lost track of what is going on outside of here, so my mask has even more to do. With all the work that my mask puts in, no one will ever see what is happening to me or what I have become. No one will ever have to see the real me.

I am all right with that to be honest. Plus, no one really needs to know. Everything that I have to handle was all created for me and me alone. Which ultimately means that the people closest to me shouldn't have to carry or even know about my burdens. So, I keep my mask on tight, until I am finally alone. When I sit in whatever space I call home, in total isolation, is when I can at last take the mask off and set it to the side. No one watching, no one that I have to protect from my inner torment, I can let it all spew out of me in a wild torrent of hidden emotion. What was once only metaphorical becoming physical in a world that doesn't belong to them. Tears soak my face and hands, coating them like a salty wet blanket. I scream into the emptiness around me as there is nothing to block the shrill sound anymore. I just let the voice degrade me, as I am too tired to attempt to deafen myself from its abuse, and my thoughts run rampant with things that suddenly become too important to let go. The monsters claw their way out of me, angry that there is no one to hurt, so they cause me pain instead. They give me physical scars with my own hands. I am too sore, yet numb, to fight anything off at this point, so I don't even bother. I have the ability to temporarily make it all go away, but I will make sacrifices when I do.

When I drink alcohol and smoke green it's like none of the things that make up my mental Alcatraz exists for a while. There is no darkness with an awful voice, rushing thoughts, or monsters. All of it stops existing for a little while. It may only be short moments in time, but I don't have to wear my mask and put on a show for the world during this time. The most important aspect of drinking and smoking is that I don't have to deal with my personal and constant nightmare for the period of time that I am not sober. I mean, I am not really myself when under the influence, but it really is for the best. I always keep the mask tucked in my back pocket, at the ready, but it's not needed for these moments. I can dance with old friends or new faces and laugh out loud at the most horrible of jokes. I am able to smile without reason and have fun without a second thought. I start to spin with the world and see things in a new perspective. I feel as though I am becoming one with who I once was. A child ready to go on an adventure at a moment's notice. It feels as though the damage of all my self-abuse never happened. Then, the feeling that I won't have to hide anymore is almost in my grasp, tantalizing my fingertips with its lies. I achingly wish that this feeling could last forever, but I also don't, as I would have to put on a show by myself without the aid of my mask, or drugs, when this moment passes. Usually when I make it to this point of comfort, I make some really bad decisions that have some equally bad consequences. The fun will cancel out those bad decisions for a while because I can't foresee the penalties of my actions while I am influenced by chemical compounds in my blood stream. My mask awaits its glorious return when all is said and done, and I will be faced with the effects of my causes.

My mask is on hand and at the ready when I wake up from any night of self-indulgence I partake in. The façade is eager to deal with the consequences caused by my debauchery from the night and early morning hours previous to me falling asleep. It will smooth talk me out of the precarious situations that I may find myself in. Then, after I make it home, it tells my friends and family, with great precision, that I only had a little fun, making very little of what actually happened. My mask isn't lying perse, it just makes sure no one knows what actually happened except for the people that were there. I naturally go back to hiding the damage from my never-ending torture from the world, like a snake slipping into a dark burrow. My mask will continue to work as it always has, putting on the performance of a lifetime, ever diligent that no one will ever know what is going on.

An unfortunate series of events happen as I start to age into adulthood. I start connecting the drinking and smoking to the way I am supposed to feel, so I start consuming these things more and more. My mask is needed to hide my actions, so no one will question what is happening and try to get me 'help'. Some people do, but nothing comes of it, as it is the wrong people questioning, and they can easily be brushed off or redirected. Then an ugly cycle brews from this, the mask in the morning and self-prescribed medication at night. I start to feel as though I need this beautiful mask more often as I am destroyed by the consequences of my actions. The cracks, bruises and scars of days passed are all hidden on the stage behind a fourth wall that my disguise won't let me see past. Not a single soul in the audience can see how much pain I am in, and what I am willing to do to dull the pain. It has become impossible to survive without hiding behind some kind of mind-altering substance or a beautifully crafted façade.

Then a day comes when I start to feel a break in my daily cycle. There is someone trying to peel off the mask, attempting to break through the fourth wall of my mask's grand performance. Carrying a backstage pass that I gave them long ago, but this time, they want to see me unmasked and unclouded. Someone that knew me before this mask put on its first show, and watched for many years after, but was never truly a fan of the work. They only want to know why I have put up a front, why I am never myself anymore, and my mask couldn't explain any of it away. They continue to try so hard to pull off the mask, and my only alternative is to shut them out. I can't let them see; they would be horrified at the disturbing mess that I have become. If they ever knew the truth, they would never be able to look at me the same again. I would only see sorrow and pity fill their eyes as they encouraged me to get help. Freeing the mask and myself from their grip creates the feeling of a door slamming between us, reverberating through years of friendship, that would change everything between us forever. Everything feels forced between us, nothing shared, causing the mask and I to perform even fiercer. Without them occasionally coming backstage, having open and less controlled conversations, and being a reminder that there was once a time that I didn't have my mask, and a daily performance. I fear I will never survive without the mask that has now become my one true friend.

A new phase begins, which brings on a completely new show, it becomes more fever pitched, and dark, very dark. I start to wonder if I ever actually lived without my mask. The time before this disguise becomes a blur. I mean, I don't think I have always had it, but I can't remember a time where I didn't have my façade covering every inch of who I am to put on a show for those I hold dear. I couldn't be grateful for all the work it puts in, and for how long it has done all that it does. The people close to me aren't upset or disgusted by what I have become. The random people in the world won't have to look at me inquisitively, wondering what is wrong with me. I can just live uncomfortably in my constant torture, positive that no one knows. My mask only asks for one thing in return, to be me. To not only be attached to the outside of me, but who I truly am. It wants to be real, so I don't have to be. It wants to be the lead actor of every show, while stay I behind the scenes, helping the show go on.

I don't know if I should make the deal, I mean really, the mask is getting the short end of the stick. Why would they want a damaged product when they can have someone greater than me? I am faced with one question, when answered, brokers a deal. With all the benefits it gives me, is everything that makes up who I am really too much to give?

Slow Poisoning

We have arrived at a tale that is incredibly intoxicating, but just as dangerous. We will see there are times when no matter how far one may have fallen into darkness, you can be ignorant to the situation. Then maybe we will learn that being oblivious to it, is not the best way to handle terribly dark things.

I drink so much alcohol so often that it goes down like water now. I turn myself into a chimney with all the green I smoke, only in the belief that it will save me from myself. I can't live life like everyone else, not anymore. The real me is too disturbed and damaged to show off. So, I hide behind a show stopping disguise about half of the time. I only have hate for myself; I don't trust anyone. When I must feel the world around me, it becomes way too much. Thoughts rushing, heart pounding, never-ending darkness and monsters completely consume me. Living life sober and out in the open isn't just hard, it is impossible. I am barely able to conversate with anyone around me without assistance from my self-prescribed medication because it is too difficult. I am incapable of taking off my mask to feel the world around me without inhaling some of that beautiful green. When morning comes, leaving my bed never happens willingly. Not without ingesting my medications the night before.

Alcohol paired with smoked green leaves becomes a molecular concoction that causes utter bliss to rush through my veins so it can quickly excite my neurons. This is the only time that I can truly laugh, smile, and express real emotions without the assistance of an elaborate facade. This 'medication' has become my crutch when I need to do something meaningful with friends and family. When I get extra liquor and green waltzing through my veins I will dance and sing the night away. With my prescription full-filled, I am ready to take on the world and experience the fun it occasionally has to offer.

I take my medication anyway I can get it: dry or sweet; fizzy or not; clean or on the rocks. I'll drink whatever. Whether it's dry brick or sticky sweet, it doesn't matter. I'll smoke it all. When I gulp down only alcohol, the world whirls around me so fast, I feel like I am dancing in the ocean. The green, alone, makes me feel completely open; the universe rushes in to fill me with new knowledge and sensations. When I consume both, I don't feel as if I am only human. I feel invincible, almost like a divine being. I feel stronger, braver, and overly confident. *The world can't hurt me. No one could reach me, no matter how hard they try. The darkness can't hold me. That voice isn't here, and my thoughts are always calm. The monsters that are constantly attacking are nowhere to be seen. I am finally free to exist as I please.* When the drugs start to wear off, I can ingest more to refresh my superhuman abilities. My goal is to keep the weight of my head off my shoulders, so I can feel a smile on my face for a little while.

As the world attempts to come down on me, I find I don't have to acknowledge the hefty problems it brings, as long as the alcohol and green are frolicking through my body. My confidence reinflating with each boost of my PRN. This makes it effortless for me to have regular conversations with random people and people I know alike. This temporary fix provides me with false bravery which stops me from being so guarded, and I don't push people away as much. This strength is the most intoxicating though. It is almost as though the weight of the world is nothing and, I can do anything and everything, but that is when the bad decisions will occur in wild succession.

I can't feel any of the dark awful things that fill my mind and my life, during the fleeting moment that my blood rushes these substances through my veins. There is no room for pain, sadness, or anger. I can only feel the smile on my face, the laugh escaping my throat, and true happiness. I haven't felt all of these amazing things since the last time I took my meds. I always make insane decisions that I will instantly regret in the morning. I try to perform tricks, which will usually make me fall or stumble, all to make everyone laugh as hard as me. I will dance around as if there is no one there to see me make a fool of myself. Then I walk to new or different places without a care in the world, staying completely unaware of my surroundings. The antics of my night will leave lingering pains that haunt me, punishing me for not thinking during my nocturnal adventures.

I begin to feel as though the universe is my playground, and I become one with everything around me. All my senses seem heightened. I search for more things to feel and enjoy. That's when I see a person who evidently notices me. They enjoy my medicated self and I hope they never have to meet what I hide or medicate away. We leave the loud and chaotic gathering to find a place for some solitude. Without the commotion of the night, their lips and hands will caress different parts of my body, even though that's not what I truly enjoy. There are specific spots that I am eagerly waiting for them to reach. I grow ever impatient as I longingly await to hit that new high that will intensify my already soaring state. If they take too long, or never bring me to that next level, I call forfeit and move on to the next person I can find. I will cycle through people, until I find the ones that can bring me to new heights, to the utter bliss that could be achieved. Sometimes sacrificing my standards to do so. My dying need to reach a higher state of being outweighs any consequence that I would face in the morning. I want to hear things from places that I could never get to in a purely physical state. I do all of this in hope to feel better longer the next day. Almost as if a time release added to the already extremely beneficial medication that I take. Not every time I take my medicine is like this, if it were, I would never be sober. I wouldn't care about the penalties to any of my actions. I would spend every day feeling this incredible, but all medications have their negative side effects. Sometimes those side effects come and go.

Life isn't always a delightful dream when I take my medication. It can all become an agonizing nightmare in an instant, and without warning. The weird part is everything starts out normal. I am drinking, and smoking, having a good time. I do my normal antics, wanting to make sure everyone is having as much fun as me. Then at some point I begin to feel heavy. The room spins and not in a good way. I can't keep myself upright, so I choose to sit. Trying to sit slowly, I drop like a rock being tossed off the pier. Once I have sunk to the bottom of my seat, I won't be able to get up on my own again. I light a cigarette knowing I will never bring the same cigarette to my lips again. My head hangs down as I become lose fabric, messily draped in my seat. I watch my cigarette burn down. I am unable to ash or smoke it. I watch the rest of the world darken around me as the cigarette snuffs out on its own. Out of the corner of my eyes I catch glimpses of people I know walking by as though there is nothing wrong with me, my paralyzed state going completely unnoticed. I physically can't speak to get anyone's attention, so I sit feeling loneliness and emptiness creep from the dark recesses of my mind. These fiendish things grip me with fear and sorrow that suffocate me as a wet blanket would. These all too familiar feelings that I was trying to hide from all along. I am completely alone in a room full of people, who have forgotten that I am here. As I watch them continue life with no need of me, I see that the world would be just fine without me. Maybe I would be missed by a few loved ones, but they would move on. They would be fine. The emptiness starts, in the place where my heart should be, and spreading to every fiber of my being until everything is gone again. I then become an unoccupied vessel waiting for my soul to come back. It never will because it is too broken and scared to return to where it originated. Now, I am left completely alone and empty for the many unsettling thoughts that I am always trying to hide from when I self-medicate.

The curious thing about it though is these thoughts aren't mine. They come from a repulsing voice in the darkness or disturbing monsters that I try so hard to hide from the world. The thoughts whirl so fast in my head that it is almost too hard to keep track of who is saying what. They are going back and forth trying to push me over an edge that I couldn't crawl to, even if I wanted to.

The monsters devilishly spit, "See, they don't need you. They don't even want you!"

The voice calmly says, "Not a care in the world for you. Almost like they would be better off without you here."

Tears threaten to escape my eyes as the monsters and the voice continue their onslaught. Still unable to move in my spot, I wish someone would finally see me. My hope resting on someone understanding where I actually am. Unfortunately, they never do. I sit there, fixating on a point in the room and stare off into space, where I lose my place in the world entirely. Spiraling down a dark rabbit hole of confusing contradictions, I am having multiple emotions all at once while being numb. I am becoming so angry that my blood boils, while simultaneously being a chilled calm. My eyes are ready to be a continuously flowing fountain of tears, at any moment, because of all the thoughts that are not mine. All the while I have a stilled indifference to it all. Only minutes may pass but to me it feels as though it has been hours, days, weeks or even years of constant torment and abuse.

In an arrogant tone, the voice says, "Worthless, utterly worthless."

The monsters, all too excited, say, "They all think you are a loser."

The voice, "Look, yet another person passes, yet you're still all alone with us."

The monsters, "You'll never escape us!"

The voice, "You know it is pointless to even hope for help at this point."

When I lose hope, I wish for my own end. Death begins to toy with me in those moments. Death sits almost out of sight, waiting to see if it will really be my time or not. Alas death is completely emotionless to my plight and only there to do what is commissioned of them. All the voices start laughing at me, because I couldn't end my life and my suffering even though that is all I want. I silently beg for the strength and the ability to finally move out of my seat so I can finally make that jump. This strength and ability are never granted. I find myself unable to get help and incapable to end it on my own. I sit and listen to the awful things from the darkest parts of my mind. Those around me are completely unaware that monsters and darkness are playing games right in front of them. Only when someone finally reaches for me, pulling me into reality, am I ultimately freed from this agony. I do whatever they ask of me, as a reward to their saving me from things unknown to them.

When I am finally able to make it back to a place where I can sleep, I let my drowsiness take hold quickly, giving no time to the dark world to torment me again. Sleep is a peaceful darkness, like laying in the middle of a forest at night. Sleep is feeling all things good and light around you without being able to see. I never want to wake up, but I always do. Remembering the side effects that my medications gave to me on nights like that, I know why people call them a poison. So, I don't drink and smoke all the time, as to lessen the chance of dealing with the side effects too often. I also have people and situations I need to be clear headed for. The fear of that place leaking into everyday life will keep me in check for now. There is always a longing to feel that freedom, and I am yearning for the ability to genuinely smile. I impatiently wait for the next time I can take my medicine, the medicine that may be leading me down a path of self-destruction. Medicines that may possibly be poisoning me sometimes giving me the ability to feel human and sometimes turning my mind into a torture chamber. Occasionally I hear the voice echo a question from the farthest points of the darkness, almost as if I am not supposed to hear it…

"How long will it take for this to finally kill you?"

Here we see how the voice of darkness and monsters make it impossible to move away from a poisonous crutch. There is one thing that will truly give you strength. That is purpose and hope. Finding what was meant to be for you and a hopeful torch to light your way through the dark. There lies your salvation from needing a crutch and finding peace within yourself.

Battered Soul Behind Strong Walls

Here we are, a place in my mind, that even I cannot enter. It is not anyone's status that prevents entrance, but pure, paralyzing fear. Constant visuals for security, and traps to bounce out anyone who dares to find a way to enter. A full fortress not for the royalty or high-class elite, but for one broken part of my mind. This piece knows only hypervigilance, fear, trauma, and self-preservation. I neglected this part for a long time, all because it was too hard to deal with. I let it control my life for a long time, without ever knowing what it truly was. Now, I give you their story, sent to me almost like an 'e-mail', as I still try to meet this part of my mind all over again.

Hello?

I am locked in tight behind walls that I have built by myself. A complete fortress that I created by hand to keep people out, to prevent them from seeing me, all to avoid getting hurt again. By keeping people at more than arm's length, I can maintain a safe existence. My only reprieves from the pain and tears are sitting alone and never letting people in. There was once a time when I wasn't here, behind walls so tall and thick. When there wasn't just darkness surrounding me as I sat alone in my bunker in the middle of my fortress. There was a time when I had nothing to fear.

So that maybe someone will understand why my fortress is here, I will share with you that joyful yet fading memory. I must tell you before my home becomes just another foreboding ruin without an explanation and I finally wither into nothing...

There was bright sunshine with open fields of flowers and grass. It was all warm and inviting, constantly building and upgrading a house as the world around me grew. Imagination was my only limitation. There was a forest to walk in and a creek with the most crisp, clean, and refreshing water. My fluid movements were in time to the sweet songs that birds sang, bees and butterflies danced in the air around me. Nighttime always brought a beautifully lit moon, a sky full of stars, and fireflies swirling through the breeze. It was all a happy place to be, absolutely perfect where problems ceased to exist. People from other worlds like mine, would come and visit. They would visit for short and occasionally long periods of time. I would even go to their worlds, which were always so different from mine but just as beautiful. Constantly having fun was a goal of mine, always in particular and peculiar ways, but fun and laughter were always the objective. I was always completely open to anyone coming over for a visit, completely unafraid of any consequences. It took longer than it should have to learn that placing complete trust in anyone was a very reckless thing to do.

The first time I was hurt in a devastating way was by someone who was supposed to be like family. A voice entered my head to tell me that this new person was my stepbrother. I had intended to treat him as nothing less than my brother. I was ready to openly love and support him as only little sisters can do. What he showed me in return was less than brotherly. I couldn't even grasp his actions as that of a human. His words hit me like snake bites, a sharp sting followed by a poison spreading a radiating pain throughout my whole form. If that wasn't enough, he destroyed the world around me, knocking down trees, polluting the water, and starting fires. The being that my realm was placed in, was also being hurt. Bruises bled into my sky and caused my world to be cast in dark ugly shadows. This was when I built my first fence, it was small and unassuming, but it did the trick. It kept him from hurting me too much, and those I called friends didn't know what was happening. Showing them only what I felt necessary, I cleaned up my domain so that the remnants of his destruction was not apparent. No one would have to worry about me. I could try to fix everything myself with no one being bothered. I visited others, in hopes that I would appear like I was before, so that no one would know or find out. *'Besides, there was no way that anyone could hurt me like he did.'* was the only thought that drove my actions at that point. I would soon learn that I was wrong. He wasn't going to be the only one that would hurt me in my life.

Soon I had to make new friends, meet new people, and experience new things. The people that came into my life, during that time, made fun of me and said hurtful things. They barreled past my fences and headed straight for me. I would rebuild my fences after every attack. They would just rip them down again, destroy everything, leaving me to rebuild from the ashes that they left behind. It was sick game to them yet a never-ending cycle of destruction for me. Their words would hit like punches. When I ignored them, they would resort to destroying my home. All of it felt like an endless battle that I would never win. It was then that I decided to start building walls. Walls would protect me better than any fence. Walls would keep people from seeing me and knowing who

I really am. This was my only choice to keep everyone from causing anymore pain. It may have been a lie, but no one could reach me which meant I was safe. My walls started small, but then grew taller, thicker, and *stronger*. As I took everything I needed from my surroundings, I turned the once lush and beautiful land around me into a barren waste land. The barren land would be covered with the expansion of my fortress. It took a long time, but every day, little by little I did it. I had made a paradise of safety and no one could penetrate it. The pride I felt was so immense that it could never be explained in words. I knew then I had finally learned; no one was to be fully trusted. There had to be layers to how far I would let people in, so I put all of my time and effort into a fortress of many walls. That is about the time I stopped seeing the light of day, and only gloomy, grey clouds hung overhead.

I layered many walls to surround my bunker, a place in the very center where I would hide for many years to watch people fail at trying to find me. I would watch the happenings throughout my fortress, always fully aware and growing more paranoid by the second. I set up traps to make sure that no one can get in. The people that I created the deeper layers for started to visit less frequently, and the traps I had set flung people out of my newly fortified home. A dark overcast, always looming, showed visitors that this was not a happy place to be anymore. No more fields of grass, flowers, forest, nor a beautiful river remained. There were definitely no birds flying, bees and butterflies danced no longer. Night was just complete darkness. No more brightly lit moon with a sky full of stars, or fireflies swirling in the air. A beautiful land that was my pride and joy was now nothing but a wasteland. All that was left was a large stronghold on top of a mountain, with nothing but cold air and dark clouds, all day and night. My friends and family kept trying to move in closer. Their attempts to try to see me, maybe even help me, all ended in vain. I met them in the layer that I allowed them to be, but I always made sure there was plenty of distance in between us. I had to ensure I had time to make a hasty escape from any potential danger. Even though they never hurt me like everyone else, it was always so hard to trust them, because if they hurt me, I would surely die.

Back in the present, I am living a solitary life, rarely leaving my bunker to meet people halfway anymore. I hide myself under cloaks when people come to see me in their attempt get a sense of where I am at now. I won't let them see the disgusting and vile creature I have become. Sunken eyes, constantly searching for the next threat in the calm darkness of my bunker. My skin, pale and papery from not seeing daylight in so long and it's covered in scars from past battles that I didn't win. Parts of my body literally disintegrating before my eyes, as if I were made of sand and my container has cracked. I know interacting with some of these people might help me, but I just can't let them actually see me now. They wonder how I am living in solitude, and how the feeling of loneliness hasn't eaten me alive yet. The only answer that I can give them slips my lips as a soft, but utterly satisfied whisper, "Why should I feel alone when I am finally safe?"

Signed,

Keeper of Memories

Traumatic things being neglected will rear their heads in ugly ways. Nightmares that wake you up with your own screams. A fear of things that make no sense. Lying to yourself and everyone else to continue not knowing the truth of the past. Memories packed away deep in the subconscious, waiting for the moment that you feel safe to be tossed about. Several years passed before the memories came back with nightmares. I would scream and yell at things that I had no control over. Memories would pop out like a jack in the box with the smallest of triggers. Panic would wash over me as I was sent back in time to a period where I was defenseless. Becoming a small child, unable to fight back against another child.

There is a note that I will leave for you. If you take a stroll through your mind, and find a fortress of immense strength, figure out who is inside before it's too late.

The Truth of Self Destruction

The last tale that this book holds is one that takes honesty with oneself to understand and overcome. Everything that you go through, all your moments and tales, can come together and create something different, yet familiar. That something can come to life, possibly become your default friend, and this can make it difficult to move forward. It's hard to see that there is something wrong, not with you but your mind. Let this tale show you that it is easy to enter here, but difficult to leave. However, I hope you hear the lesson at the end and take it to heart.

While I was alone, I was never truly alone. When everyone would leave and they would become fed up with me, it only *seemed* I was completely alone. That was when my thoughts would come out to play. My thoughts would begin to spill out of me when they knew they would have me all to themselves, then they turned into a being all their own. It was like someone would be with me always. They had their own voice, and they would tell me all kinds of things. They would speak in firm tones to try and correct my behavior.

They would say things like, "You know that you should have done better with this today?" I always believed there was no way they could be wrong. I could have done better with whatever they would mention. Everything I ever did was inadequate because I was never good enough for anything. The raised voice of my thoughts rang through clearly to respond, "You are good for absolutely nothing, do you understand that? Good for nothing and completely worthless."

They continued, "You realize how wrong you were today, like every day. Just completely wrong. Will you ever learn to do anything right?" Again, my thoughts were not wrong, like I always was. No matter how hard I would try, and no matter what I would do, I was always wrong. Everything I would do was just the wrong thing to do. I would always fail unless I could somehow figure out how to be right.

The worst thing that my thoughts would talk to me about, the topic that would hurt the most… "Are you just going to let your life fall apart again? I swear to God, you just want to create more work for me. Do you realize how difficult it is to deal with you?" My thoughts were not wrong. My life would just topple over like a game of Jenga and I would always crumble with it. No matter what I did or tried, the life that I had made would just fall apart without any warning. Every time, like a cycle, I would have to rebuild from the rubble and ash. Although I couldn't hold my life or myself together long enough to make a difference, my thoughts would always be there to help put me back together again.

Now, I know what all of you are going to say, **"How could you listen to that?"** *Or maybe,* **"How could you just believe that about yourself?"** *I will reiterate. I knew no other way. What I know now and what I knew then are two very different things. My only belief was everything that my thoughts would say, and I understood nothing else about myself. So, no matter how awful the thoughts were, it was all I could hear when I was alone. I felt like I had no one to talk to. Do not worry, the lesson hasn't been learned yet, and the only way to do that is to finish the story.*

I would just sit and listen to everything that my thoughts would have to say. I was unable to discern how awful those things were that were being said. I could only believe that my thoughts that surrounded me, like a hovering parent, would only say these things because they wanted to help me. They wanted to change me into something better and if that was the goal, how could that be a bad thing? I always thought that being anything else would have been better than what I was. Plus, why would my thoughts spend all this time trying to make me better if they weren't good for me? How could this have been such a terrible thing for me if it were all to improve what I was? I never could bring myself to believe that they were wrong.

It was so much easier to believe that I could have done better. I believed that I should have made everything perfect before I put it out in the world. Anything less was just pointless to do. I could only see me doing everything wrong. I couldn't believe I let failure even be an option for me. If I could just hold myself together long enough, life would finally be good for once. Then, I wouldn't burden everyone around me with my unstable nature. I just had to figure out how to do things the way they are supposed to be done. I would stop failing at everything I did and suck it up and hold myself together no matter how much it hurts.

Everything I felt I needed to do would create an immense pressure. I would try and use this pressure to hold myself together. I would do what I could to increase the tension, so there would be more of it to use. The pressure intensified until I felt as though I was at the bottom of the ocean, unable to move or breathe, being crushed under the weight of all the stress I had created for myself. The pressure that I had made would only last for a little bit each time before everything would fall apart. The life that I had worked so hard to rebuild would fall all around me. It would crash like an ocean wave of rubble, and loud booms would sound with the demolition. I would begin to crumble like I was made of sand. Then, I would mix with the rubble of my life. I was indistinguishable with the destruction that I was surrounded by.

My body is completely broken and unable to get up. My thoughts would rush in. They were always at the ready to berate me, while putting me back together again in the same breath. As they sorted through everything to find pieces that made up who I was, they would point out everything I did wrong. My thoughts would tell me how this was my fault, and that it has always been my fault. I only get put back together enough to continue putting together the puzzle that is me, still being criticized as my thoughts supervise my progress. I would be told that I barely deserved the help that I got, and I should be grateful that I wasn't left alone to pick myself up. I could never apologize and thank my thoughts enough for them helping me. Being forced to bring myself together should have taught me a lesson, but I never could quite learn what that was.

'Do not let people help' was my motto. I couldn't let people see me like that, as it wouldn't have been fair to them. I couldn't let them help because the reality of my worthlessness would be exposed. All I wanted was to be good enough, so that meant I had to do this on my own. I had to learn from my mistakes. So, I would put up with the rude and demeaning comments because my thoughts were the only being that I could accept help from. My thoughts slapped me in the face with their harsh reality, and I would let them because I believed that I deserved so much worse. I was so grateful to them for always being there like they promised. They promised me they would stay with me always, so long as I would always listen to everything that they had to say. So, I made a promise that I never thought I'd have to break.

I figured that if I was never alone that I would finally be better. I felt, if I could listen to my thoughts hard enough and take in everything that they said, I could finally be a better person. A person that deserved to have people in their life. People kept coming into my life, and it was always so much easier to push them away. I didn't deserve to have many friends because I wasn't good enough yet. There were people that stayed, they seemed to care a lot about me. I tried to push them away, and they wouldn't leave. They'd always tell me that my thoughts weren't normal or natural. They told me to not listen to them. That I'd feel better if I stopped listening to them. I explained that I couldn't, that shutting out the thoughts was nearly impossible, and I couldn't do it alone. Very few stayed, which I still wish that I could have seen that they had been there.

Though, many of those people told me that I needed to grow up or that I was being ridiculous. Then, they would leave, and I would be left alone with my thoughts.

My thoughts would say things like:

"Of course, they left, you were only dragging them down."

"You're not good enough for *real* friends."

"They would just ruin all your progress. You want to finally be good enough, right?"

"You don't need friends; you only need us."

I couldn't fight my thoughts because I believed that they were right. I knew that I would just bring the ones I cared about down with me. The first time they noticed my life falling apart in an almost synchronized demolition, they'd most likely be scared off. They would run away so fast that it would almost seem as though they were never there. My thoughts would rush in like always because I would truly be all alone again.

The last time my life fell apart, I had achieved more in rebuilding than all the times before. I thought it wouldn't happen again. I thought I was finally better, but I wasn't. This time was different though. As I fell to my knees under the enormous pressure that general stress created this time, I thought I saw a person. As everything I built fell and I crumbled under my own weight, I looked past the dust and rubble to see I was wrong. There wasn't just one person; there were multiple. They watched everything topple on what was an unstable foundation, and they never left. They stood and watched, waiting until they could come in. My thoughts racing to be first, I watched as these people screamed to tell me that they were there. My thoughts tried to keep me deaf to their words and blinded to their form. It wouldn't work that time because that time was so very different and changed every aspect of my life.

I called for help. The first time in a long time, I called for help from a person, from real people. My thoughts were infuriated, screaming:

"How dare you!"

"I can't believe this!"

"You don't need them, you need us! Only we can put you together!"

However, I wanted to try. I needed to try something new. When the people finally made it to me, my thoughts turned silent. They began to help me but myself together. Sure, it was a long process and there were some mistakes made, but everything came back together again…eventually. I saw a silver lining emerge from the dark clouds that was my life. There was a new hope when everything had finally come together. It was a torch in the dark.

That's when I realized that their intention was always to help. They had always been there and had never left, but my thoughts made it too dark to see them, always rushing through me like immense waves to keep me from hearing them. I put up towering barriers to keep them out. I always had a mask on to make them think that I was okay. I may not have done everything myself, but some things I did because I thought I was protecting myself and others. The things that I thought were protecting me, were only protecting my thoughts, allowing them to do whatever they pleased with me. My thoughts have always wanted and continue to want me on unstable ground to give them plenty of leverage so their manipulation can grow and fester.

I realized that I was forcibly trying to build my life, when I should have been letting it grow organically. I also realized that I was continuously building on unstable ground, making it impossible to have a life that I truly wanted. This was, however, making it easier for the things in my head to continue to torment me. Now I finally know, and I hope you do as well. Self-destruction is only possible with self-sabotage. You are the only one who can find it within yourself to acknowledge it and get help. You are the only one that can end the cycle of rebuilding on unstable ground. Let your life grow instead of trying to build it. Hear the people around you and let them help cultivate the right place for the real you to grow. Finally, see what life is, rather than what you are told it should be. You are the catalyst to your own self-growth.

To whom it may concern:

I started out many letters like that. Especially near the end when I thought there wasn't anything to live for. When I didn't have any hope for my life, and I could see nothing but despair in my future. The last note I started like that, before this one, I finished it with:

I just couldn't anymore. I'm sorry.

Love always,

Shela

That was going to be the last thing I had ever said to the world. Some of you will shame me, some of you will understand, and there will be plenty that will fall somewhere in between those. There were a few times that I wrote a bunch of long letters to a multitude of people, but then I thought I was just hurting more people with the lengthy letters. I wrote these final thoughts because I had hit a certain point multiple times where I believed that I didn't have a future. I had no hope and believed that I was a burden to my close friends and family. I would write these notes before I did anything because they deserved an apology for my actions. Even if I couldn't get the words out, they deserved to know that I was sorry for everything that I had ever done, and what I was going to do.

I knew then, as much as I know now, that ending my own life was going to hurt them, and that they would grieve the end of my time here on earth. On the other hand, what outweighed this pain was that I felt as though I was bringing them down with me. That I was somehow going to drag them down with me into the deep dark abyss that I was completely lost in. The only way I could think to save them was to kill myself. I never talked about what I was going through because I was afraid of causing them pain or discomfort with me not being ok. I gave them a front so they wouldn't have to worry. I put up walls to keep new people out. I drank and smoked to keep the monsters and the pain away as best as I could. This only made me fall deeper into the cold unforgiving ground. When I hit rock bottom, I just kept digging, because facing and talking about my problems was too much to bear.

I didn't want to see a therapist of any sort because I was terrified about what they would do to me. I had an irrational fear that they would drug me up, toss me in a padded room and throw away the key. Which granted, was completely irrational, but a real and serious fear that I had. I had stopped writing, painting, crafting, all the things that I did for fun, and just focused on being functional at work, and getting home to whatever alcohol I had in the fridge that night. I was just barely existing when I wrote that last letter that started this note. When I went out that night, I was going to end everything. The living of a fake existence, pretending to be happy so no one would have to pity me. Sleeping around so that I could feel something other than a painful numbness. Drinking and smoking to feel like a child again. Walking down the street with a bottle of pills on my person, I opened it up and went to take it when a friend messaged me. I honestly couldn't be more grateful for that message because I wouldn't be here today, writing this book and note for you to read.

I cried more than I ever had that night, I wanted it all to stop. I just wanted to feel *normal*. I begged and I pleaded for the answer. I hoped that if whatever higher power out there was actually listening this time would finally answer my cries for help. I put it all out there. If there really was a reason for all of this, I wanted the answer now. Most of all, I just wanted it to end. I wanted it all to feel better. If I wasn't allowed to end my life, then give me a reason to be here. About a month and a half after that, just when I thought that I wasn't going to get my answers, I found out I was pregnant. I was with a guy that I shouldn't have been with once but stupidly decided it was a good idea to try it for a second time. He didn't want any part of the pregnancy, even though he lied and told me that he did. I know, ha-ha on me, right? Well, I went through the whole pregnancy mostly alone. This is when I realized, my friends and family knew more than I had ever thought. I knew then that I shouldn't have been going this whole thing alone and should have let them in a long time ago. This is when I started writing again.

My mind finally unclouded from everything, and for the first time in a long time, I didn't want to die. I may not have wanted the child I was carrying while I was pregnant, but I knew I had to exist for at least for a little while longer. When I had my son though, my whole life changed. I finally felt whole. I know it will sound weird, but it is like he is one of my soulmates. It felt as though he knew me my whole life and maybe even a few others before this one. I knew, in that moment, he was given to me in this life to help me move forward and give me the hope I had lost so many years before. That is kind of when this book began.

As I said, I started writing again while I was pregnant, but I wasn't really doing anything substantial. I guess I was just getting back into the swing of things. After I had him, I started writing little stories that had actual feeling to them, real substance. So, I continued doing just that, little poems, very short stories until my son had just turned three and I looked at a story I wrote, and wondered, '*Sure I put a poem or two up for a contest, but would someone actually read this, and maybe, get help?*' That thought had never occurred to me before. I never thought that anything I wrote would be good enough for someone to want to read. I was always so timid about things that I wrote that this thought had never truly came to me before. Something this time said, "*Yes, this*" I rolled with it. I started to flesh it out, and just let the universe decide things for me. I posted on Facebook and found my incredible editor Stacy Reppel. Then I went looking around for illustrator for the book and couldn't be more enthused with the outcome that my longtime family friend Brenda Wirthman did all the artwork on the inside of the book.

(The editor and illustrator mentioned in the beginning of the book are not getting enough credit. They are beyond amazing, and this book would not be anything without both of them. Please, go back to the first pages, look them up online, and give them the love and attention that they rightfully deserve.)

This whole writing process has taught me a lot. Like, it is ok to ask for help and therapy isn't so scary. Seriously, I have grown a lot because of everything

I had to do to make this book happen. I talk to people and get on them to do their work as much as I do mine. I worked hard to pull people together to make a collaborative project. I listen to people now when they say they are proud of me instead of just laughing it off. Most importantly, I learned that I really could do whatever I put my mind to. Which is honestly something I never would have believed about myself. This newfound belief in myself is an indescribable feeling. There was a lot of tears, and literal jumping for joys, that I would never be able to fully convey in any author's note. I have a whole new lease on life, and my little muse goblin is ready to abuse me while giving me new triumphs, and I am ready for it all.

Now we're here, me writing this long-winded author's note. If you've made it to this point. You are probably wondering if there is a final piece of advice or a lesson to be learned from this long note. I am here to tell you, there really isn't. Your journey will be different from mine, so there is not one straight answer. I will say though, if any of this resonated with you, if you felt any of this within the deepest part of your soul, please seek help. It may start with just reaching out to a close confidant, telling them how you feel. You may find that prescription medication is what you need, or maybe just talk therapy, which is totally cool too. Seriously, there is no good reason for you to be going through this alone. If you took anything away from this book, let it be that it is ok to ask for help. Always remember when you feel lost or broken, you are not alone.

Love and light your way,

Shela Hutchinson

P.S. After this, there is a page with helpful numbers and websites for you to check out when your own head is bringing you down. Be safe out there everyone.

National Suicide Prevention Lifeline:
800-273-8255

American Foundation for Suicide Prevention:
https://afsp.org/

Crisis Text Line:
Text things like, 'Talk', 'Home', 'Hello', to 741 741

Information on the Crisis Text Line:
https://www.crisistextline.org/